SIMPLE SOLUTIONS®

Tricks for Treats

PLUS TRAINING TIPS

BY JEAN M. FOGLE

BOWTIE
PRESS®

A Division of BowTie, Inc.
Irvine, CA

VP, Chief Content Officer: June Kikuchi
VP, Kennel Club Books: Andrew DePrisco
Production Supervisor: Jessica Jaensch
Production Coordinator: Tracy Burns

Art Director: Jerome Callens
BowTie Press: Jennifer Calvert, Amy Deputato, Lindsay Hanks, Karen Julian, Elizabeth L. McCaughey, Roger Sipe, Jarelle S. Stein

Library of Congress Cataloging-in-Publication Data
Fogle, Jean M., 1952–
    Tricks for treats : plus training tips / by Jean M Fogle.
        p. cm. — (Simple solutions)
    Includes bibliographical references and index.
    ISBN 978-1-935484-22-6 (alk. paper)
    1. Dogs—Training. I. Title.
    SF431.F652 2010
    636.7'0887—dc22
                                2009041816

BowTie Press®
A Division of BowTie, Inc.
3 Burroughs, Irvine, California 92618

Printed and bound in China
14 13 12 11 10   3 4 5 6 7 8 9 10

SIMPLE SOLUTIONS®

Tricks *for* Treats

PLUS TRAINING TIPS

dog

Contents

Tackling
Tricks

hat builds brain power, exercises your dog, and is guaranteed fun for the both of you? Trick training! Young or old, big or small, dogs enjoy trick training. Molly, my Jack Russell Terrier, and I have trained for many different canine activities, but trick training remains our favorite. Done in short sessions, it gives your dog the attention that he deserves and the mental and physical stimulation he craves. Through the need for mutual cooperation, trick training builds a better bond between you and your dog. It also teaches your dog how to think, how to puzzle out solutions, and best of all, how to have fun with you. Seeing your dog thinking—trying to figure out what the silly human is asking him to do—is the best part of trick training. The AH-HA moment is priceless.

There are several rules you must follow to ensure that trick training is successful. One of the most important is that you must mark the *exact* moment your dog performs the action you are trying to teach him. To mark the moment, you can use a clicker or a particular word, such as *yes*. Whatever you choose, work on getting your timing down, so you mark the action you need for the trick. While training Molly to growl on command, I happened to say "Yes" right as she was growling and backing up. Now when I ask her to growl, she backs up too!

Here are eight other important rules for trick training.

1. **Choose the right treats.** Don't be tempted to use your dog's dinner kibble; find a treat that will really motivate him (such as cheese, chicken, or hot dogs), and use it only for trick training. Cut or break the treat into small pieces.

2. **Understand the trick thoroughly.** Read all the directions before you begin a trick, and make certain that you really understand them before you start training. Be sure to study the photos accompanying each trick in this book.

3. **Assemble all the components you need for the trick beforehand.** Have the treats handy so you can quickly reward a job well done. If you need any props (such as a blanket or a leash), make sure you have them ready as well.

4. **Train in short sessions.** Learn how long your dog will stay focused during a training session, and quit each lesson while you are ahead.

5. **Fade the lure quickly.** If you use a lure (a treat) to motivate your dog in the beginning, be sure to *fade* the lure as soon as possible. Once he understands the trick, use treats less and less often, until you no longer need a lure at all.

6. **Break the trick down, if necessary.** If you get stuck, try dividing the trick into smaller steps, and make the sessions shorter until you get a breakthrough.

7. **End on a positive note.** Happy dogs learn better. End the session with something your dog performs well so you can give him an enthusiastic "Yes!" and a big reward.

8. **Most of all, be patient and have fun!**

Gracious Greetings

What is friendlier than a welcoming handshake (or pawshake) or a wave hello? Your dog can learn to do both in no time. Traditionally, *shake* was taught by grabbing a dog's leg and pumping it up and down. Instead, use a treat to lure your dog to lean to one side so his paw naturally comes up on its own. The *wave* builds on the *shake*.

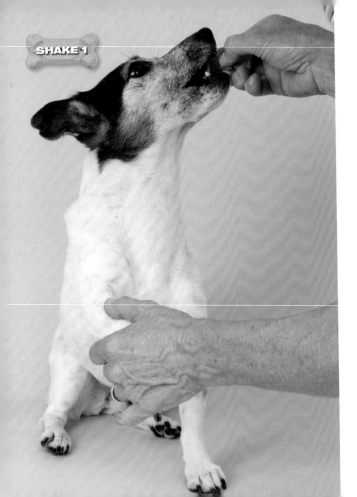

Shake

Have your dog sit in front of you.
Put a treat in your right hand, and
hold your hand directly in front of
his nose. Slowly move your hand
to the right. He will follow the
treat's scent with his body, which
will unbalance him, causing him
to lift his right leg off the ground.
Gently take his leg in your left
hand, say "Yes," and give him the
treat (*Shake 1*). Repeat luring with
the treat in your hand until your
dog begins to anticipate what you
are doing. Now, instead of luring
with a treat in your right hand,
offer your left hand to him, palm

SHAKE 2

up (*Shake 2*). Most dogs understand that you still want to handle their paws. Now you can name, or label, the trick *shake* for the dog. Before you know it, just saying "Shake" will have your dog giving you his paw.

Don't hold the treat too far away when you lure us to lift a paw, or we will be tempted to lunge forward instead of leaning sideways. And some of us are left-pawed, so if your dog seems to have trouble, try getting him to lift his left paw instead of his right.

Molly's Tip

Wave

For the *wave*, start with your dog sitting in front of you. Warm him up by reminding him how to shake. This time, move your hand up higher than you usually do for *shake* so your dog is reaching up to get to your hand. When he swipes at it, tell him "Yes" and give him a treat. Once your dog is reaching up, you can label his movement *wave* (*Wave 1*). The hand signal for

wave is made with your palm tilted downward and your fingers curled up (*Wave 2*); a wiggle of the fingers signals *wave*. Once your dog understands *wave*, move from standing or kneeling in front of him to doing so beside him. Take it slowly, and go back to a previous step if necessary. In the end, you want to stand by his side so you both can wave hello to your adoring fans.

Take It
Or
Leave It

ake it and *leave it* are two basic cues your dog needs to know before he can move on to the more complicated tricks. They involve training him to take any object you ask him to and, conversely, to resist snatching up even the most tempting treat until you give your permission. *Take the tissue* is a fun trick to teach after your dog learns the *take it* cue.

Take It

The first step is an easy one: just put a treat in your hand, and as you show the treat to your dog, say "Take it" (*Take it 1*). Repeat several times, presenting the treat and telling him to "Take it" each time. Your dog will soon associate the phrase *take it* with taking the treat from your hand.

TAKE IT 2

Now find a small toy or stuffed animal your dog plays with. Hold it in your hand as you did the treat, and ask him to "Take it." If he ignores it, give it a shake. The second he takes it (*Take it 2*), give him a lot of praise and treats. Train him to take a variety of objects, from a set of keys to his leash.

Leave It

Start off with your dog sitting in front of you. Have a treat in each hand, close your fingers around them, then place your right hand on your chest and your left hand behind your back. Move your closed right hand in front of your dog's nose, and say "Leave it." He will sniff, lick, and possibly paw at your hand. The second he stops trying to get the treat and either looks at you or backs away, say "Yes" and give him the treat in your left hand. Continue doing this until he knows to leave the hand holding the treat in front of him (the right one) alone.

Once he ignores your closed right hand, say "Leave it" as you open that hand to expose the treat in front of him. If he lunges for the food,

close your hand so he can't get it. Don't say anything, just wait until he looks at you (*Leave it 1*), then say "Yes" and give him a treat from your left hand. Your dog must learn that even with the food exposed, *leave it* means he must not take the treat. Once he is able to leave the treat when it is exposed in your hand, you can lower the treat to the floor and ask him to "Leave it" (*Leave it 2*). If your dog lunges toward the treat, block him with your hand so he understands this is the same trick, just in a new position. Now, instead of giving him a treat from your left hand, you can say "Yes" and let him eat the treat on the floor as his reward.

TAKE THE
TISSUE 1

Take the Tissue

Here's a trick that utilizes the *take it* cue. Begin with a tissue in your hand, and tell your dog "Take it" (*Take the tissue 1*). Any touch of the tissue should be rewarded. Work up to the point at which he grabs the tissue in his mouth. Once he is eagerly taking the tissue, introduce the tissue box. Pull a tissue out of the box, and fold it several times to make it easier for him to grab. Reinsert it in the box loosely so your dog can pull it out with ease. Now hold the box, and say "Take the tissue." When he does so, say "Yes" and give him a big treat.

Now that he knows how to take the tissue, you want to have him bring it to you. Place the tissue on the floor close to you. Ask him to "Take it," and put your hand out to receive it. The second it is in your hand, say "Yes" and give him a treat. Now begin to place the tissue farther away from you, gradually increasing the distance. If your dog drops the tissue before bringing it to you, remind him to take it, and only give him a treat when the tissue is in your hand.

Once he understands how to bring the tissue to you, use double-sided tape to secure the tissue box to the floor, then pull a tissue partway out of it. Stay close to the box, shake the tissue, and encourage your dog to take it. Put your hand out for the tissue, and when he gives it to you, say "Yes" and give him a treat. Gradually increase the distance from the box to you. Now you can begin to introduce the *sneeze* command. When you get the tissue box out, say "Take the tissue" and add a big fake sneeze. Soon you can drop the words and just sneeze; your apparently considerate dog will then trot off to get you a tissue (*Take the tissue 2*).

Molly's Tip Be prepared for soggy, shredded tissues; I have discovered that these tissues just don't hold up to canine teeth and slobber.

Going,
Going,
Gone

The three movement tricks *go around*, *go through*, and *go over* are fairly easy for you to teach and for your dog to master. With *go around*, dogs learn to work away from their owners and move around various objects; with *go through*, dogs learn to navigate tunnels. *Go over* is especially easy to learn because dogs naturally love to jump!

Go Around

For this trick, use a small orange cone (pylon) or box for your dog to go around. To begin, have him sit on your left side (*Go around 1*). Place a treat in your right hand, show it to your dog, and use it to lure him to circle the object as you say "Go around" (*Go around 2*). Once he gets around the object, say "Yes" and give him the treat. Continue to lure, saying "Yes" and treating once he gets around. If you are having trouble, you might try sending your dog around counter-clockwise. Most dogs favor one direction, and finding his favorite one will make the trick easier to teach successfully.

Now, while standing close to the object, ask your dog to go around without using the lure. Most dogs catch on that it's the same game and they will get the treat once they go around. When your dog has done so, move back a bit, and ask him to "Go around." Say "Yes" when he does, but wait until he returns to you to treat him. Use the instructions to teach him to go around from your right side. Work on increasing the distance, and have him go around different objects.

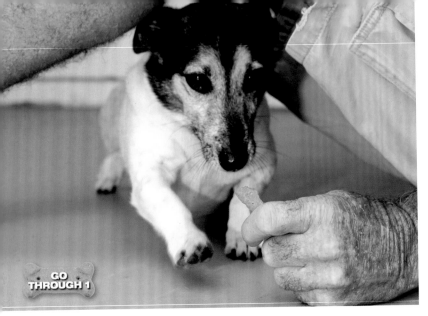

GO THROUGH 1

Go Through

For an easy way to teach *go through*, sit on the floor and lift your knees to a level that allows your dog to crawl under your legs. (If your dog is too large for this method, go directly to the tunnel exercise described on page 29.) Have your dog lie down so he is facing the arch you have made with your legs. Show him a treat by reaching through your legs from the other side. Using the treat as a lure, tell him "Go through" (*Go through 1*). Reward him when he does. After luring a few times, you should be able to get him to crawl under your legs without the treat. Once your dog gets the idea of the *go through* cue, you can

SIMPLE SOLUTIONS

move on to using a play tunnel (sold at toy stores). Start with a short tunnel, one your dog can see through from one end to the other. Have someone hold him at the entrance while you move

GO THROUGH 2

to stand at the exit with a treat. Now tell your dog to "Go through." The second he does, say "Yes" and give him a reward. Once he goes through the short tunnel with confidence, begin to lengthen the tunnel, and then upgrade to a curved structure (*Go through 2*). If the tunnel curves too much, your dog might be reluctant to go through, so make it a slight curve at first, then gradually work up to a sharper one.

Go Over

Start with a stick, a broom, or a bar on the ground, and ask your dog to walk over it with you (*Go over 1*). Say "Over" when he steps over the bar, then say "Yes" and give him a reward. Once you've repeated this a few times, use bricks or other sturdy objects to prop up the bar so he will have to step a little higher to go over it. When he does, say "Yes" and give him a treat. Repeat a few times until your dog readily responds to the cue. Next, raise the bar higher still, and instead of stepping over it with your dog, stand at one end of the bar, toss the treat over it, and say "Over." When he jumps, say "Yes" and give him a treat.

Continue raising the bar until he is actually jumping (small hurdles can be purchased at sports stores for this trick). Now have him sit next to you while you stand behind the bar. Show him a treat, then throw it over the bar while telling him "Over." (*Go over 2*). Once he is comfortable jumping over the bar, you can teach him to jump over other objects.

Molly's Tip

If you have a puppy, check with your veterinarian to be sure it is safe to teach him a trick that entails jumping. Puppies need to be a certain age before you begin training them to jump, so they don't risk tissue injuries.

Spinning Circles and Crawling Around

f you have ever watched dancing with dogs (also known as canine freestyle) or seen trick dog competitions on television, you will recognize these two tricks. *Circle* is when a dog spins around like a top, and *crawl* looks like an army maneuver. Both are fun to teach.

Circle

Start with your dog in front of you. Have a treat in your hand, and hold it so he can see where it goes (*Circle 1*). Move the treat to the right, encouraging him to follow it. Circle the treat back toward his tail, then around until your hand is in front of you again. The second he completes the circle, say "Yes" and give him the treat. Make sure he can see the treat, and go slowly enough for him to follow it with his nose. Where his nose goes, his body will follow (*Circle 2*). You can begin saying "Circle" now when he turns. To

drop the lure, you can pretend the treat is still in your hand and make the same motion you did before. When he completes the circle, give him a treat and lots of praise! Make the circle smaller with your hand until you are using just a finger to outline a circle. Now you can have him circle with the voice command or the hand signal.

If you want your dog to turn in a circle to the left instead of the right, you can use the same techniques in the opposite direction and use the cue *spin* instead of *circle*. Just don't let him get carried away circling or spinning until he's dizzy!

Molly's Tip

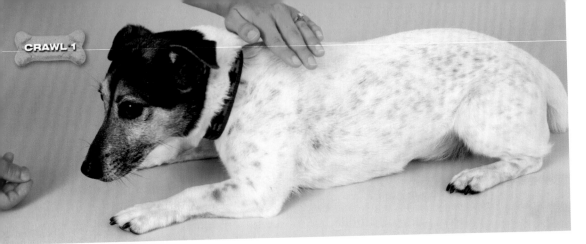

Crawl

Get your treats, and tell your dog "Down." Now squat in front of him with a treat in one hand. Position your other hand over his shoulder (*Crawl 1*). Hold the treat level with his nose—if you hold it any higher, it will cause him to pop up to get the treat, which you don't want. Let him sniff the treat, then move it just out of his reach so he must stretch to get to your hand. You are looking for any tiny creeping movement forward. The second he creeps, say "Yes" and give him the treat (*Crawl 2*). If he pops up, tell him "Down," and begin again. Continue keeping the treat just out

SIMPLE SOLUTIONS

CRAWL 2

Molly's Tip

Teach the crawling trick on the carpet or grass, so we can perform it more easily and without hurting ourselves.

of his reach, rewarding each creeping movement. This is when most people make a mistake by increasing the distance too soon. Once your dog is crawling, don't move too fast or move your hand with the treat too far out of his reach; this can cause him to pop up to get the treat. Take it slow, and end the session before he loses interest. Once he is crawling some, add the word *crawl* to label the trick. The goal is to get him to move forward with his body low to the ground.

Rolling
on a Rug

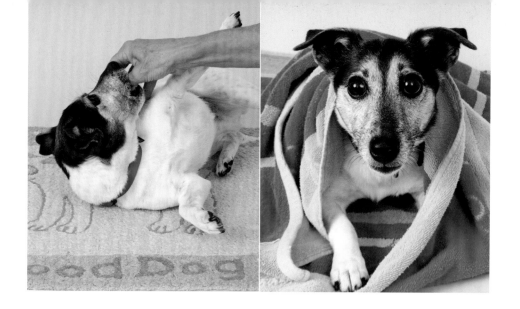

Roll over is another basic canine trick, one of the feats that most people like to teach to their dogs. *Roll over* is also an essential component in the "awwww"-inducing trick that it is known as *cover the baby*.

Roll Over

Have a handful of treats ready, and ask your dog to lie down in front of you. As he relaxes, pay attention to which hip he settles on. If he is resting on his right hip, he is already leaning to the right, making it easier for him to roll that way (*Roll over 1*). Let him see the treat, then hold it above his left ear. Slowly move the hand with the treat over the back of his head to the left. His head will move with the food, and his body should follow. Say

"Yes" and give him a treat (*Roll over 2*). If your dog doesn't roll over following the treat, you may need to guide him by gently pushing his top front leg in the roll's direction. Once he is rolling over with the lure, add the cue *roll over*. Now, fade the lure, and use a hand signal to cue him. I use my index finger to indicate a rollover.

Molly's Tip

Always do this trick on a rug or outside on the grass, so we have a soft place to roll over. If your older dog is reluctant to roll over, he may have a sore back. Check with your veterinarian if it seems like a serious problem.

Cover the Baby

Spread a beach towel on a soft surface. Have your dog lie down on a third of the towel (you want there to be enough towel to actually cover him). Pick up an edge of the towel, draw it close to him, and ask him to "Take it." When he grasps it, say "Yes" and give him a treat (*Cover the baby 1*). Use high-value treats (such as hot dog pieces) to get him excited about this trick. Repeat these actions until he is

 COVER THE BABY 2

eagerly taking the towel. Now when he takes it, quickly ask him to "Roll over." Most dogs are excited enough by this point to roll over with the towel in their mouths, thereby *covering the baby* (*Cover the baby 2*). You can now label the trick *cover the baby*. If your dog drops the towel, go back to the *take it* cue, and instead of giving your dog a treat the second he grasps the towel, wait a bit to get him to hold on to it longer.

A Touch of Paws

Y ou could say the tricks *touch* and *paws up* go hand in paw. *Touch* is simply having your dog touch your hand. He can do so with his paw or with his nose, although many beginners find a nose touch easiest to teach. *Paws up* is also simple. By eight weeks of age, Molly knew how to sit with her paws up so we gave the trick that label.

TOUCH 1

Touch

Have your dog sit in front of you. Move your hand, palm first, toward your dog's nose. Curious dogs will reach over and touch your hand (*Touch 1*). The second he touches your hand, say "Yes" and give him a treat. If he just sits and looks at your hand, put a tiny bit of peanut butter on your palm. When he touches it to get the peanut butter, say "Yes" and give him a treat. Do this for a while, but then gradually wean him off the peanut butter. Once your dog is touching your hand with confidence, begin moving your hand around, up and down, right and left. Keep your voice happy, and offer lots of praise. When you are certain your dog understands what you are asking for, add the word *touch* right before he touches your hand. You want him to associate the word with the action. Now walk away a few steps, show him your hand, and ask him to "Touch" (*Touch 2*). When he moves to touch your hand, give him a jackpot of treats. If he won't come over to touch, you need to move closer to him and repeat your earlier actions until he really understands what you are doing. Remember to keep your training sessions short and stop while your dog is ahead and having fun. Some dogs will take several sessions to catch on.

TOUCH 2

Paws Up

Ask your dog to sit, and hold a treat slightly above his nose (*Paws up 1*). If he jumps for the treat, tell him to "Sit," and try again. Most dogs will lift up their front paws in an attempt to get the treat (*Paws up 2*). Once he is balanced, say "Yes" and give him the treat. After he does *paws up*, drop the lure, and label the trick. If your dog has hip or back problems, then skip this trick as it may be painful and could worsen his ailment.

PAWS UP
2

Molly's Tip

Once we know how to do *paws up*, be prepared for us to do it all the time. Our lovely eyes will beseech you to give us some treats!

Open and Shut

O pen the door utilizes the *take it* cue. *Shut the door*, which never fails to impress guests, is based on the *touch* cue. For these tricks, find a door that swings easily and is not too heavy for your dog to open or shut. Molly began on a kitchen cabinet door and later moved on to larger doors.

Open the Door

To make training this trick easy, begin with the door ajar. Hold a tug toy or soft leash in your hand, and ask your dog to "Take it" (*Open the door 1*). When he takes it, say "Yes" and give him a treat. If he won't take it, entice him by shaking the leash like a toy. Once he is taking it from your hand, tie the leash to the doorknob, and tell him to "Take it" again. Because the leash is no longer in your hand, you might have to shake it once more before he will grasp it. When the door begins to open (*Open the door 2*), say "Yes" and give your dog a treat. Once he is doing that, wait to reward him until he gives a bigger tug on the rope, which helps swing the door open. Now you can label the trick *open the door*.

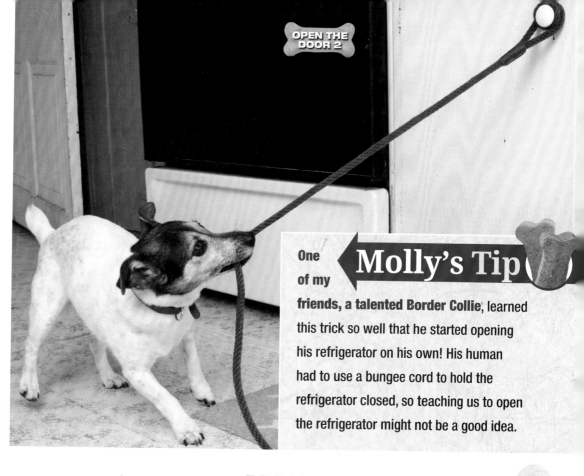

OPEN THE DOOR 2

Molly's Tip

One of my friends, a talented Border Collie, learned this trick so well that he started opening his refrigerator on his own! His human had to use a bungee cord to hold the refrigerator closed, so teaching us to open the refrigerator might not be a good idea.

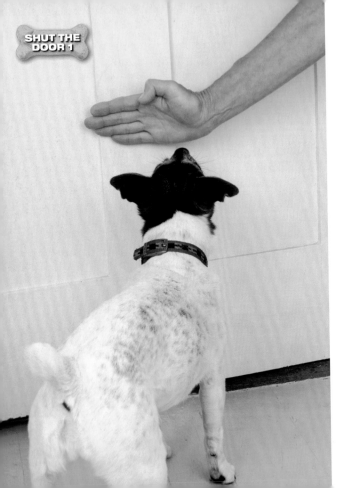

Shut the Door

Molly shuts the door with a paw touch instead of a nose touch, but you can have your dog do either. Warm your dog up by moving around and asking for touches to your hand. Open the door, place your hand in front of it, and ask him to "Touch" your hand (*Shut the door 1*). Do this several times, then take your hand away and ask for a touch, pointing at the door. The second he touches the door (*Shut the door 2*), say "Yes" and give him a big treat. For dogs who are reluctant to touch the door, go back to the peanut butter trick. A little dab on the door is enough. When he reaches forward and touches the door for the peanut butter, say "Yes" and reward him. Fade the peanut butter just as before. Once your dog is reliably touching the door, you can add the cue *shut the door*. Move back from the door a little with your dog, and ask him to "Shut the door." His racing forward to touch the door should help swing it shut. If he is reluctant to move over to the door, bring out the peanut butter again, then fade it out once he gets the hang of the trick.

Tiskets, Taskets, and Toys

Does your dog always greet you with a toy in his mouth? Does he carry his toys around from room to room? If so, you should have no problem training him to perform the tricks *take the basket* and *put away your toy.*

Take the Basket

For this trick, use a basket that your dog can easily pick up. Begin by having him sit in front of you. Hold the handle close to his mouth, and ask him to "Take it." The second his mouth touches the handle (*Take the basket 1*), say "Yes" and give a treat. Let him get used to the feel of the handle in his mouth. Next, lower the basket to the floor, and ask him to "Take it." At this point, you can label this *take the basket*. Slowly add distance, and you can ask him to get the basket and bring it to you. Now begin walking as he brings the basket, letting him carry it for a few steps beside you (*Take the basket 2*), then reward him. He will soon realize he has to come along with the basket to get his treat. If you and your dog are of a musical bent, you might teach him to pick up the basket when you start humming "A Tisket, a Tasket." Using a green and yellow basket would also be a nice touch!

TAKE THE
BASKET 2

Put Away Your Toy

Start by holding a toy and asking your dog to "Take it." Reward and repeat so he is reminded of the cue. Place the toy on the ground, then ask him to "Take it" and bring it to you. When he drops it into your hand, say "Yes" and reward him with a yummy treat.

Now find a container or bin that your dog can use as a toy box. Show him a ball, a stuffed animal, or another plaything to pick up, then place your hand over the container so he can deliver the toy to you. When he drops it into your hand, say "Yes"

PUT AWAY
YOUR TOY 2

and give him a big reward. Once he is consistently dropping the toy into your hand, withdraw your hand so the toy will fall into the bin (*Put away your toy 1*). Say "Yes" and reward your dog the instant he drops the object into the toy box (*Put away your toy 2*). Now you can label the trick *put away your toy*.

I have been known to carry a toy around, hoping my human will ask me to put it away so I can get a treat. Funny that she couldn't get her kids to pick up their toys, but she expects me to work for my dinner. Go figure!

Molly's Tip

A Deeper Bond

By the time you finish teaching your dog these tricks, you will notice a definite difference. When you get the treats out, he will be eagerly waiting for a signal and may even offer tricks before you start. Your dog will be better able to solve puzzles, and best of all, the bond between the two of you will become much deeper.

Acknowledgments

I want to thank Molly for teaching me everything I know about dogs. She has been a fantastic teacher, ever patient and forgiving of my mistakes. She has taught me to embrace new experiences, forge ahead without fear, and best of all, to live in the moment. Dogs give us so much but ask so little; enjoy each day with yours!

About the Author

Jean M. Fogle lives in Fort Valley, Virginia, and has written about dogs since she got Molly in 1997. Her photos have appeared in books, magazines, and calendars. She is the author of *Salty Dogs*, a photo book of dogs at the beach, published by Wiley. Visit her Web site at www.jeanmfogle.com and her blog www.pixels-n-pen.blogspot.com.

SIMPLE SOLUTIONS®

Tricks for Treats

Want a dog who can wrap himself snugly in a blanket, put away his toys, and leap over hurdles? In *Tricks for Treats*, step-by-step instructions and photos—as well as training tips from a savvy terrier—tell you how to teach your dog to perform these impressive feats and many more. Trick training will also deepen the bond between you and your pet and make you the talk of the dog park!

The Simple Solutions® series is brought to you by DOG FANCY® magazine, the world's most widely read dog magazine. Stay up to date on all things dog by logging on to DogChannel.com.

ISBN 978-193548422-6

$6.95 US/$7.95 CAN

BOWTIE PRESS®

A DIVISION OF BOWTIE, INC.
3 BURROUGHS, IRVINE, CA 92618